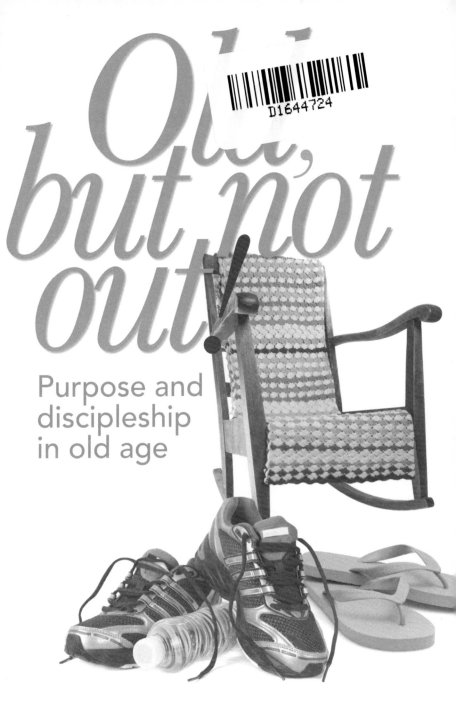

Old, but not out

Purpose and discipleship in old age

James Taylor

DayOne

ISBN 978-1-84625-306-5

British Library Cataloguing in Publication Data available

Published by Day One Publications
Ryelands Road, Leominster, HR6 8NZ
Telephone 01568 613 740   FAX 01568 611 473

email—sales@dayone.co.uk
web site—www.dayone.co.uk

Cover design by Wayne McMaster
Printed by Orchard Press Cheltenham Ltd

OLD, BUT NOT OUT!

Commendations

Here is a book 'for such a time as this'. To an increasingly ageing culture, and its church component not least, Jim Taylor confronts the special issues of the 'senior' years with typical thoughtfulness, biblical insight, and pastoral relevance. *Old, but not out!* should find a place in every church bookstall, and on every concerned Christian's bookshelf. It is a worthy legacy from a highly esteemed and fondly remembered Christian leader, who personally embodied so much of what he writes here.
—Rev. Dr. Bruce Milne, author, and former Senior Minister of First Baptist Church, Vancouver, Canada.

I enthusiastically commend this delightful book on living a God-centred and meaningful life in old age. There is no book on the market that quite achieves what this book does. Through careful reflection on key biblical characters in old age and through astute personal insight, Jim Taylor offers great dignity and meaning for 'third agers'. The book is typical of the author: witty, carefully measured, pastorally insightful, impressively illustrated and spiritually warm.

It is a book for all who are concerned about the loss of hope and purpose for retired people. I lent it to my elderly father (ninety next birthday) who has been a Christian leader for nearly seventy of those years. He read it with great enthusiasm and said he is going to use it as a basis for starting a Bible Study group in his old people's home!

But it is a book not just for older people. As the proportion of elderly people in our population rapidly increases, all who are involved pastorally should read it. It is a great resource for pastors, pastoral care teams and preachers. It is an outstanding example of the fact that the richest pastoral theology is that which emerges from a lifetime of service to others.

—Rev Andrew Rollinson, Minister of the Baptist Church in St Andrews, Scotland

(Andrew Rollinson has been a Baptist Minister for thirty years serving in churches in Newcastle-upon-Tyne, Edinburgh, and in St Andrews. As Ministry Advisor to the Baptist Union of Scotland, he worked alongside the late Rev Jim Taylor in supporting retired ministers and their spouses.)

Contents

Introduction

What follows had a twofold origin. It really began with the formation in my previous church of a fellowship of older members and friends, to which my wife and I were invited. We did the usual things when we met; there were talks, demonstrations and, of course, we ate together. What was impressive was the response. The conversations did not major on problems; far from it. Instead, we discovered the joy of fellowship with those who had also entered the 'third age' of life. We had a series of Bible studies in which the contributions were delightfully uninhibited! The first series of four, for which I was responsible, looked at some biblical characters who were of advanced years or some passages of Scripture which seemed particularly relevant to where we now were.

Also, following my retirement from pastoral ministry, my wife and I were involved in the coming together of retired ministers and their spouses in our denomination in Scotland. We met regularly simply to talk together, to enjoy one another's company, to eat together and, most of all, to engage in mutual encouragement. Many acknowledged that, since retirement, they had experienced loneliness or a loss of identity, even a feeling of uselessness. Some admitted that, after the early euphoria, they were not really at ease with retirement from what had been so central, even dominating, in their lives. Many, if not all, experienced relief when they realized that the difficulties they were wrestling with were not uncommon. One of the inevitable conclusions we reached was that even Christians, with many years of service, preaching and pastoral care behind them, needed the reassurance that God still had a purpose for their lives. Retirement was not the end.

Those who attended these groups had long lived with the conviction that the Bible has something of relevance for every stage of life. So what did it have to say to those who had been active and deeply involved in their churches but now sensed that they were regarded, by the state certainly and often by younger Christians, as of pensionable age? Did it have anything to say to those who were becoming aware of their growing limitations, or who were feeling that everything worthwhile in their lives belonged to the past?

What follows was therefore born and, like Topsy, continued to grow. No evidence will be found in God's Word for the suspicion that retirement or older years are synonyms for 'being put out to grass', or that they are an excuse just to sit back with weary resignation. This book is written to encourage or, in the language of the day, to stimulate positive thinking about being a bit older than others. Dare we hope, too, that younger Christians, and particularly Christian leaders who have retired people within their orbits, will appreciate an insight into the situation facing those who were once where they are and now feel redundant?

1 The example of Abraham and Sarah

We start with Abraham, or, as he was called earlier in his life, Abram. When he was a comparatively young man, God had called him out of Ur, away from his home country, his people and his father's household (Gen. 12:1). He had responded 'by faith', but the Promised Land turned out to be a learning experience. His textbook, which he had to learn, was the nature of the God he was called to obey. It was all summed up in God's name, 'the LORD', a name which implied power, authority and sovereignty. Abram was a quick learner. Several times we hear him addressing his God as 'O Sovereign LORD' (Gen. 15:2, 8). A unique and remarkable covenant was established between this Sovereign Lord and Abram, a covenant which was breathtaking in its promises and was to be equally powerful in its implications. Not only was Abram to have a son, but his offspring would be as numerous as the stars in the heavens. The land, too, would be the inheritance of those who were prepared to trust God. Abram, now renamed Abraham, was required to walk before God in faith and obedience. God's promise was simple but profound in its implications: 'I will … be your God' (Gen. 17:7).

TRUST IN GOD'S PROMISES

Forget for a moment the problems which were to follow. Everything is right for Abraham as we enter the story. The God whom he has obeyed is sovereign, is ready to bless him in unimagined ways, and will be with him in a bonded and secure relationship.

Such is also the situation of the believing Christian. The sovereign God of Abraham is our God. In his grace, he has called us. Great and precious promises are ours. The bond, or the covenant, between us and our God has been sealed by a death—the death of God's own Son on the cross. We are heirs of this new covenant. Life may have its troubles, and antagonisms have to be faced, but peace comes when we trust our God, daily looking for his grace, guidance, strength and reassurance. We are remarkably like Abraham at the beginning of our story.

The years passed, however, for Abraham and his wife. No heir appeared, nor was it likely. It was, in fact, impossible. The passing years had taken their toll. When one reached their age, there was an impressive list of impossibilities, not just difficulties, and child-bearing was one of them. There was little use harbouring dreams and aspirations. They had to be realistic. The days of productive usefulness were past.

No one could reasonably blame Abraham and Sarah for feeling like that, now that Abraham was one year short of a century (Gen. 17:1). They could well have been thinking or talking about it. It would have been strange if they didn't ponder what might have been.

THREE VISITORS

One day, however, three unexpected visitors arrived (Gen. 18). There was a certain mystery about them. Naturally, hospitality had to be offered and was graciously accepted. Then came the bombshell: 'I will surely return to you about this time next year, and Sarah your wife will have a son' (Gen. 18:10). Sarah laughed. She had heard it all, listening as she was at the entrance of the tent. The very suggestion was laughable, even preposterous. She and her husband were past it. Such things as the visitors suggested belonged to those younger and more energetic. Despite the earlier promises, the days of playing an active role in them were gone.

It all sounded so unrealistic; and we, in turn, are encouraged by so much in our pressured society and the culture it has spawned to laugh with Sarah. In our later years, we are almost conditioned to be 'realistic' and come to terms with our limitations.

However, one thing is sure. Unless we have escaped to a desert island, there is no lack—in our society at large, in our own community and in the church—of challenges, opportunities, open doors and beckoning responsibilities. What is to be our response, as older people? Is it to be indifference, a shrug of the shoulders or even laughter? If laughter, it comes in the guise of 'We're not up to it any more!', 'At our age, we don't have the energy!',

'We're simply past it!' or 'It's a job for younger, fresher minds!'

Sometimes, the challenge can be very ordinary—something, indeed, which can be easily coped with by someone younger, very often a grandchild! The computer on my desk used to have a dial-up Internet connection. That meant that while I was wrestling with e-mails, I couldn't use my phone. The answer was to ask BT for broadband. Several times during the installation I wished that I had never started! After the struggle of following all the instructions, my screen appeared to be a jungle of icons, tabs and further instructions. My response was laughter: 'This is impossible! I'm not up to this any more! O, for a simple typewriter!'

NEW CHALLENGES

We all face the demands and complexities of life today. Even the challenge of having to understand modern thought and cultural changes makes us feel like giving up the struggle and resigning ourselves to undemanding novels and TV soaps. Books that threaten to challenge a mind rapidly growing stiff and rusty are neglected or, if begun, are soon laid aside for something lighter. We know, for example, that in order to communicate in a postmodern world (and we're not very sure what that is), we are going to have to change our approach, style and even vocabulary. We feel we are not up to it, and we give up the struggle. But what we are really doing is laughing—not with the laughter of humour, but with the laughter of resignation and unbelief. The words of an unknown author are apt: 'We use the matter of our old age as an excuse for not relying on the power of God.'

Zechariah, who was, with his wife, 'well along in years' (Luke 1:7) reacted very similarly to Abraham and Sarah when told of Elizabeth's forthcoming pregnancy. 'Zechariah asked the angel, "How can I be sure of this? I am an old man and my wife is well along in years"' (Luke 1:18). Yet Abraham and Sarah had to learn a lesson. They ought to have realized that, though they had undoubtedly aged, God remained the Sovereign Lord who had called them and made great promises. 'Is anything too hard for the LORD?' (Gen. 18:14) was both an assurance and a rebuke. It silenced laughter.

Most of us, even if we claim to be mature,

experienced Christians, often deserve the same rebuke. There is no age limitation when it comes to claiming God's promises, relying on his power and entering into full possession of Christ's riches. The promises of God are greater than our willingness to claim them.

The wonderful truth is that many older Christians have faced enormous challenges and have not laughed. They have refused to use their advancing years as an excuse for neglecting God's call. C. T. Studd was one such. He served his Lord in China for ten years as a missionary followed by six years in the USA. He founded the Heart of Africa Mission, now known as Worldwide Evangelisation for Christ (WEC), serving in Belgian Congo until he died. Many another would, at some point, have pleaded ill-health or old age and thrown in the towel. He left his attitude of mind in the motto of WEC: 'If Jesus Christ be God and died for me, no sacrifice can be too great for me to make for him.'

Jennie V. Hughes was another. Her age when she went to China in the 1920s is unknown but she, too, refused to let human weakness keep her back. Her initial reaction was, 'Is God really calling? China is no place for a single woman missionary!' She then read in Job 26:7, 'God suspends the earth over nothing.' She clearly felt God saying to her, 'You say you are nothing. If I can hang the earth upon nothing, don't you believe that I can do something with you, even in China?'

RETIRING OFTEN

One of the impressive features of our age is the number of people who have retired from their profession or trade and then offered themselves for Christian service overseas, even for a few years. They could have retired comfortably and settled back, resisting all challenges if not with a laugh, then with an amused smile. Two friends of mine, both highly qualified nurses, have 'retired' five times. The first retirement was from their careers in the UK; the others were from spells in Kenya and Uganda training student nurses. Each spell was expected to be the last, but, faced with new challenges, they headed back in obedience, refusing to allow age or undoubted weakness to hinder them. To some it seemed impossible that at their age they could cope with the climate and the challenges, but they did so, as they claimed God's strength and his undoubted promises. As William Booth said, 'God loves with a great love the man [or woman] whose heart is bursting with a passion for the impossible.'[1]

Alfred Lord Tennyson gives the following lines to Ulysses as he broods over what he might do for an encore, having seen the world:

Though much is taken, much abides; and though
We are not now that strength which in old days
Moved earth and heaven, that which we are, we are—
One equal temper of heroic hearts,
Made weak by time and fate, but strong in will
To strive, to seek, to find, and not to yield.[2]

So, old age and retirement are no excuse. There is no room for unbelieving laughter. If God calls us and backs us by his promises, we can face what at first sight is beyond us with expectation and exhilaration.

Notes

1 Quoted at www.allthingswilliam.com/passion.html; accessed August 2012.

2 **Alfred Lord Tennyson** (1809–1892), 'Ulysses', 1842, ll. 65–70; available at www.eecs.harvard.edu/~keith/poems/Ulysses.html; accessed August 2012.

OLD, BUT NOT OUT!

2 The example of Caleb

I n his earlier years, Lord Randolph Churchill, the father of Sir Winston Churchill, showed exceptional giftedness and was regarded as having great promise for the future. These gifts, however, rapidly declined and his powers dramatically and sadly faded.

To a greater or lesser extent, and for a variety of reasons, this is physically, and often mentally, true of all of us. Over time we find that we start needing spectacles for reading, that we take longer over what was once simple, that problems daunt us a little more and that our memory gradually becomes sluggish. Old age is making its presence felt, often gradually but sometimes suddenly.

An older Christian once confessed to me, 'I no longer have the energy I once had for Christian service!' So, is our physical or mental decline paralleled by a spiritual decline? We may find ourselves content to spectate on the Christian scene rather than participate, to talk in preference to acting. Instead of welcoming change, we are beginning to be content with things as they are. Rather than challenge every problem, we try to ignore them. We begin to talk of being 'realistic' and prefer to let the young people get on with it. Our day is over, or nearly so!

If that is our depressing attitude, we have a great deal to learn from a remarkable Old Testament character, Caleb.

CONFLICTING ASSESSMENTS

We first meet Caleb as Israel is camped at Kadesh Barnea, almost on the threshold of the Promised Land. The story is told in Numbers 13. The forty-year-old Caleb, Joshua and ten others were sent to spy out the land and see if it lived up to the promises of God. In the event, all twelve agreed that the land was worth possessing and that all God said about it was true. 'We went into the land to which you sent us, and it does flow with milk and honey!' (Num. 13:27). They also produced some of its fruit, to remove all doubt. The majority recommendation, however, caused a stir.

Ten of the twelve said, 'Don't let's go up! The opposition is too strong! There are too many obstacles and problems!' Only Joshua and Caleb felt otherwise.

The ten assessed the problems in the light of their own weaknesses and limitations. 'But the people who live there are powerful, and the cities are fortified and very large … We seemed like grasshoppers in our own eyes, and we looked the same to them' (13:28, 33). By contrast, Caleb and Joshua assessed the undoubted problems in the light of the promises and power of God. 'We should go up and take possession of the land, for we can certainly do it' (13:30). These two contrasting attitudes are alive and well among God's people centuries later.

We begin to see the contrast when we consider the different reactions to the world we seek to win and the culture we seek to penetrate. Some Christians accept the commission of our Lord to witness but are overwhelmed by the complexities of a postmodern society; others see it as a great challenge. Some major on the seemingly widespread indifference to Christian things, while

OLD, BUT NOT OUT!

others see the opportunities and openings. Some are obsessed with the weakness and confusion of the modern church, while others stress the power of the gospel to save and the empowerment of the Holy Spirit.

There is a story about the War Cabinet during one of the darkest periods of the Second World War. The Prime Minister, Winston Churchill, outlined the desperate situation. Britain stood alone against the might of Nazi Germany. Some present expressed despair and counselled negotiation with the enemy. Churchill's response was to say, 'Gentlemen, I find it all rather inspiring!'[1] Caleb and Joshua would have found that response rather congenial!

OUR OWN WEAKNESS

We also see this contrast when we dwell on the inadequacy of our own lives. If we insist on honesty or realism, we know that 'Not many of you were wise by human standards; not many were influential' (1 Cor. 1:26). We can see, quite clearly, our own personal inadequacies and weaknesses, the limitations of our understanding and our stumbling, bumbling ways. 'Who are we to attempt great things for God?' we might ask ourselves. We are so like the ten spies who believed that they looked like grasshoppers! A sense of fatal resignation, a feeling of complete impotence, envelops us as we face the challenges of modern society, the masses lost to the contemporary church, the addicts, the bewildered and the confused. We see, as our Lord did, the sheep without a shepherd, but our attitude suggests that we don't really believe there can be a shepherd. There's nothing that can be done, certainly not by us—or so we think.

The Calebs of this world, however, believe with Paul that 'we have this treasure in jars of clay to show that this all-surpassing power is from God and not from us' (2 Cor. 4:7). The parallel in the New Testament is the story of Peter and John confronting the challenge of the lame man at the temple gates in Acts 3. 'Silver or gold I do not have, but what I have I give you. In the name of Jesus Christ of Nazareth, walk!' (Acts 3:6). Those like Caleb in our generation may not have the trappings of worldly power or the impressive resources of the state, but they can say to weary and broken men and women, 'In the name of Christ, your problem is overcome!' Christians, along with this good man of old, can possess, in our daunting age, the God-given assurance and confidence that others similar to the ten spies lack.

GOD'S PROMISE

Caleb and Joshua insisted that they had been given a very special promise and that that was the secret of their confidence. 'And do not be afraid of the people of the land, because we will swallow them up. Their protection is gone, but the LORD is with us. Do not be afraid of them' (Num. 14:9). That promise, or assurance, was to lodge in Caleb's mind for a further forty-five years of desert wandering with God's people. Surely those long, weary years would dim his vision and blunt his faith?

We could understand it if that happened, because something like it is the experience of most of us. There is a great deal about modern life that tends to dampen our glow, take the edge off our faith and blunt our initial enthusiasm. We may have responsibilities that exhaust our commitment and drain our vitality. The older we get, the easier it is to lose our spark! We admire the energetic commitment we see in younger Christians and read about in popular Christian success stories. For us, however, it increasingly belongs to the past. There are always pressures, even within Christian circles, to keep us safe and conventional. The passing years take their insidious toll and we leave the conquering of mountains to those who are younger and who have the energy we once had but have no more. We then sit back.

Not so Caleb! The passing of years, even as they were spent wandering about in the desert, had done nothing to dim his zeal and his determination. He had hung on to the promise God had made and he would not let go. Not for him the resignation which the years tend to bring. One writer has said,

Even at his ripe old age, Caleb was not ready for a rocking chair or a tent in some retirement village in the Jordan Valley. Some may have thought that it was the time for his disengagement from life, but he claimed a mountain. He

OLD, BUT NOT OUT!

asked for a challenge, not a cushion. He wanted more adventures in his 'retirement' years.[2]

NO RETIREMENT

Caleb is a rebuke to all who, in their senior years, are prepared to sit back and allow others to possess God's land. There's no retirement in the life of faith! First, he reminded Joshua that, in contrast to the ten, he had 'followed the LORD [his] God wholeheartedly' (Josh. 14:8). That was history. He had been forty years old then, full of, if not youthful vigour, then middle-aged zeal and determination. Then came the crunch:

So here I am today, eighty-five years old! I am still as strong today as the day Moses sent me out; I'm just as vigorous to go out to battle now as I was then. Now give me this hill country that the LORD promised me that day. You yourself heard then that the Anakites were there and their cities were large and fortified, but, the LORD helping me, I will drive them out just as he said. (14:10b–12)

A promise God had made had sustained him, overcoming the debilitating passing of the years and

OLD, BUT NOT OUT!

the arguments about leaving it all to the up-and-coming youngsters. 'Not a man of this evil generation shall see the good land I swore to give your forefathers, except Caleb son of Jephunneh. He will see it, and I will give him and his descendants the land he set his feet on, because he followed the LORD wholeheartedly' (Deut. 1:35–36).

Such faith and resolution are a rebuke to those of us who are nearer eighty-five than forty and feel that the retirement age from active Christian service is lower than the pensionable age. We may not be allowed to hire a car after seventy-five, and we may be regarded as 'yesterday's man/woman' after we pass sixty, but God welcomes the attitude and faith of a Caleb. Faith like his is sustained not by gazing at the desert and lamenting the passing of the years, but by dwelling on God's Word, truth, promises and nature. Martin Luther is reputed to have said. 'I rubbed God's ears with his promises', and when it comes to that activity, we are not debarred by age!

The trouble with the majority of the Israelites was that they had little sense of the purposes of their sovereign, all-powerful God. Their

OLD, BUT NOT OUT!

commitment to entering Canaan was therefore half-hearted and easily disturbed. They angered God by their grumbling, complaining ways. 'You grumbled in your tents and said, "The LORD ... brought us out of Egypt to deliver us into the hands of the Amorites to destroy us"' (Deut. 1:27). No wonder God said, 'No one who has treated me with contempt will ever see [the land]' (Num. 14:23).

Caleb stood out from that majority by his faith in God's leading purpose. 'But because my servant Caleb has a different spirit and follows me wholeheartedly, I will bring him into the land' (Num. 14:24).

Are many Christians saying, in effect, 'What point is there in being committed to a lost cause?' If we follow less than wholeheartedly, lacking the faith of Caleb, we are really saying, 'God is not all-powerful. His cause is merely drifting along! God, too, is confused and baffled by the modern scene!' If, however, we are convinced of God's sovereignty and controlling purpose, even in a world such as we see around us, our faith cannot help being resolute and our commitment undimmed by the passing years.

OLD, BUT NOT OUT!

An older hymn has us singing 'Fading is the worldling's pleasure'.[3] For the majority, the years certainly bring decline, increasing weakness and a certain resignation to, and acceptance of, things as they are. The Christian in the mould of Caleb, however, no matter the date on the birth certificate, goes from strength to strength. 'Though outwardly we are wasting away, yet inwardly we are being renewed day by day' (2 Cor. 4:16). Our confidence and faith become more robust as we grasp and claim the promises of a sovereign God.

Notes

1   Quoted in **William Barclay,** *The Letter to the Romans* (Louisville, KY: Westminster John Knox Press, 1955), p. 234.

2   **Richard Morgan,** *I Never Found That Rocking Chair*, quoted by **Paul Beasley-Murray** in 'Faith at Fifty: Older People, Gospel and Church', *Ministry Today*, June 2003; available at ministrytoday.org.uk/magazine/issues/28/332/; accessed August 2012.

3   **John Newton,** 'Glorious Things of Thee Are Spoken', 1779.

3 The example of Naomi and Ruth

Mothers-in-law are in short supply in the Bible. There appear to be only two. Simon Peter had a mother-in-law. The time when she was 'in bed with a fever' (Mark 1:30) was the occasion for a miracle of healing. After serving the band of disciples she disappears from the scene, never to be mentioned again. The other mother-in-law is, of course, Naomi, whose story appears in the book named after one of her daughters-in-law, Ruth.

When we are introduced to her, Naomi's situation is quite dire, and yet it must be replicated thousands of times in the modern world. Her story, therefore, has a strange relevance centuries after it was first enacted.

Along with her husband, Elimelech, and her two sons Mahlon and Kilion, Naomi became the equivalent of an economic migrant. Their home was in Bethlehem in Judah, but the trouble was that there was nothing to eat. 'In the days when the judges ruled, there was a famine in the land' (Ruth 1:1). So they left and went to Moab. That was almost unthinkable for a group of God's people. Moab was the enemy. When, long before, Israel had sought permission to travel along 'the King's Highway', Moab had refused right of passage (Judg. 11:17). In the days of the judges, the king of Moab had invaded Israelite lands as far as Jericho and oppressed Israel for eighteen years. Later, the prophets were to be severe on Moab, promising nothing but judgement. Still Naomi and her family went. Better a slightly hostile reception than starvation.

TRAGEDY UPON TRAGEDY

Then disaster struck. Naomi's husband died. It would have been different if she had remained in Bethlehem. Hebrew legislation had always been considerate where widows, along with the fatherless and strangers, were concerned. She was, however, in a foreign land. To heap tragedy upon tragedy, her two sons, who had married Moabite women, Orpah and Ruth, also died.

If the book of Ruth is, when you read it to the very end, a story of God's providence, then the opening scene is the dark side of that providence. Naomi's situation could not have been worse. Husband, two sons—all gone. Alone, with two young widowed daughters-in-law, she was in a strange and largely hostile environment.

She decided to go back to Bethlehem. At least she had heard that the famine had passed (Ruth 1:6). Did she hesitate over taking these two young women back, knowing the general state of the country? The historian had graphically summed up the situation: 'In those days Israel had no king; everyone did as he saw fit' (Judg. 21:25).

Naomi was poverty-stricken. She was widowed. She was going back to a disturbed society where lawlessness, anarchy and violence raged. She was going out of the frying pan into the fire. She was wise in giving the two younger women a way out. 'Go back, each of you, to your mother's home' (Ruth 1:8). There was nothing but kindness and appreciation in Naomi's attitude towards them. She would face her future alone. She would have to; there was no real alternative. She would lie awake at night thinking of what had been and what might have been, of happy family days and sudden partings, of her own loneliness and her relatives by marriage now far away.

It is not difficult to find parallels in modern life for Naomi's situation. I think readily of a couple who, following the husband's retirement from business in the city, moved to the seaside, anticipating years of each other's company. Family had long since gone their own way and lived far away. Suddenly and unexpectedly, however, the husband died and financial provision for the future turned out to be less than satisfactory. The widow couldn't drive, the shops were some distance away and she was, as yet, not well known by anyone in her new town. These same circumstances are repeated time without number, even in Christian circles. Every pastor could quote several Naomi-type situations, or variations of the same, from his own experience.

HUMAN FEELINGS

How do the Naomis of the world react to such situations? If we were writing Naomi's story and felt in a pious frame of mind, we would have her saying things like, 'The bumps are what you climb on! It's one big adventure! Come with me, dear Orpah and Ruth, and accept the challenge!' But Naomi spoke honestly. 'It is more bitter for me than for you, because the LORD's hand has gone out against me!' (Ruth 1:13). This woman, whose name meant 'pleasant', 'lovely' or 'beautiful', now said, 'Don't call me Naomi … Call me Mara, because the Almighty has made my life very bitter. I went away full, but the LORD has brought me back empty. Why call me Naomi? The LORD has afflicted me; the Almighty has brought misfortune upon me' (1:20–21). It is significant that, in all this, she used the name of God that signified his covenant relationship of faithfulness to his people. She was recognizing, even in her sorrow, that all that had happened to her had happened, in some mysterious way, in God's sovereign will and purpose. Her reaction, however, was very human. She made no attempt to hide her feelings of anger, grief and bitterness.

Many a Christian goes through a bitter experience akin to that of Naomi and experiences very human feelings, and yet clings to the belief that God is in control and knows what he is doing. It is difficult for a stranger to faith to understand that, but it is true. The elderly, bereaved, lonely Christian can say, 'I know God is almighty and I can leave the explanation, even the responsibility, for this bitter experience in his hands.'

At least two biblical illustrations come to mind. Job had lost everything—wife, family, livestock. His friends had numerous unhelpful suggestions as to the cause and how he should react. Yet he was able to say, 'Though He slay me, yet will I trust Him' (Job 13:15, NKJV). Joseph had been treated dreadfully by his brothers, was the innocent victim of scurrilous accusations and was let down by those who had promised much. Yet things turned out well for him, even if his prosperity and status were in a foreign land. When his guilty brothers, the perpetrators of his initial plight, stood before him in justifiable fear, he was able to say, 'But God sent me ahead of you to preserve for you a remnant on earth and to save your lives by a great deliverance. So then, it was not you who sent me here, but God' (Gen. 45:7–8). What a difference the word 'but' makes when you describe your situation, however dark, and trust in the presence and purposes of a faithful God!

Henri Nouwen tells a story in a slightly different context that has relevance. 'There was a man on a horse galloping swiftly along the road. An old friend standing in the fields, seeing him pass by, called out "Hey rider, where are you going?" The rider turned round and shouted back, "Don't ask me, just ask my horse!"'[1] Is that not the reaction of those who feel that things are going badly and they have lost control of their circumstances? God is considered irrelevant. Too often, for the majority, it is the horse that is in control. For Naomi, and those who trust in the way she did, while not minimizing the gravity of their situations, they know that their almighty God is in charge. That conviction makes all the difference.

FAMILY RELATIONSHIPS

Another facet of Naomi's story that is of interest to those who are older is her relationship to her sons' widows, Orpah and Ruth—two much younger women. Orpah wished to be a wife again and so, given the opportunity, returned to Moab. Ruth wished to remain a daughter-in-law and returned with Naomi to an unknown and potentially difficult situation in Bethlehem. We have to use our imaginations a little, but the evidence points to a lovely, caring relationship between the older Naomi and the younger Ruth. We look in vain for mother-in-law/daughter-in-law tensions—there are none. The relationship between these two women, who differed in age, cultural background and religious upbringing, seems to have been completely harmonious.

It is not always so when there is a disparity in age. We hear a great deal today of the 'generation gap', a gap which, all too often, seems impossible to cross and is the source of innumerable tensions and domestic and social crises. Media reports tell us how older people are afraid not just of 'hoodies', but of any group of young folk wandering the streets. Parents and children lose touch, fail to understand one another, seldom share matters of mutual importance and often appear to live on different planets. And then we have the mother-in-law stories, which are intended to be humorous but

OLD, BUT NOT OUT!

really hide the creaking, if not the breakdown, of a potentially valuable relationship.

Helen Oppenheimer has interesting comments to make in the book *Spirituality and Ageing*:

Making friends between generations needs more effort than making friends with contemporaries. One starts with fewer shared assumptions. It may be like making friends with foreigners. There is a new language to be learnt, at least to comprehend, even though one would feel foolish to try to speak it. It is mildly embarrassing if Granny starts to say, 'That's cool'; and, by the time Granny has learnt to say it, that particular expression is probably out of date. What matters is not keeping up with trends, but refusing to settle down lazily in unexamined assumptions.

Making friends with people much younger than oneself offers opportunities, not only to enjoy their company, but also to let them see that the old ones too are human beings, with distinctive characteristics, likes and dislikes, weaknesses and achievements.[2]

Does not an elderly widow, or widower for that matter, often feel lonely even when daughters-in-law visit dutifully but fail to share and appreciate her situation? It needn't be so. Naomi and Ruth could be models for a loving, caring relationship between young and old. At one stage, my church encouraged young students to 'adopt' an older person living alone. At first, on both sides, there were hesitations. 'What shall we have in common?', 'What shall we talk about?', 'I'm out of touch with today's youth!', 'Will an old lady be interested in what I do with my friends?' Yet the result was invariably the forging of a deep and lasting relationship with mutual benefit. Naomi and Ruth are alive and well, even in our modern world.

A much-neglected ministry in many of our churches is that of the older members towards the younger. It should not be so. The older members, with their experience and age, have much to give to those who are slowly finding their way and often feel so vulnerable and unsure. Elizabeth, the elderly mother of John the Baptist, was a great encouragement to the very much younger Mary, who was soon to give birth to the Messiah. Paul, nearing the end of his life, had much to give to young Timothy, who was painfully aware of his youthful timidity. How this cross-generational ministry can be encouraged in a local church should be one of the challenges addressed by those in pastoral leadership. They should find among the older members a willingness to adopt not a superior, 'we've been there before' attitude, but a warm accepting love towards, and interest in, the younger members of the congregation. Ruth and Naomi encourage us to bridge the gap between the generations, the building material being love.

Notes

1   **Henri Nouwen,** *Creative Ministry* (New York: Image Books, 1978), p. 3.

2   'Inner Resources for Growing Older', in **Albert Jewell,** (ed.), *Spirituality and Ageing* (London/Philadelphia: Jessica Kingsley, 1999), p. 44.

OLD, BUT NOT OUT!

4 The lesson of Eli

It is said that the older you get, the more tolerant you become. There are exceptions, of course, but as a generalization it may be true. Age tends to soften the hard edges of judgement. Black is no longer as black as it used to be, and no longer is every moral issue either black or white. The older perhaps more experienced mind begins to discover that there are lots of greys around. The firm stand you once took over some issue may be something that, if you don't exactly regret, you doubt whether you would repeat. You become a little more understanding of the shortcomings in others which you once vigorously condemned. Perhaps, as the years advance, you develop a deeper understanding of the frailties of human nature and the bizarre behaviour of your fellows. Your experience of the world is greater and, in any case, you now lack the energy, even the motivation, to follow up words with actions. All that—which sounds very reasonable—is simply an excuse for inaction or a growing tolerance towards what was once treated with firm rejection. Most older people will empathize with that scenario.

All this leads us to think of Eli. He appears in the early chapters of 1 Samuel as God's priest in Shiloh and as a judge over Israel. Those who have a casual acquaintance with the Old Testament will associate him with the boy Samuel and the voice of God in the temple at night. At least Eli had the sensitivity to realize that the voice Samuel heard was that of God. Eugene Peterson, in his *The Jesus Way*, is perhaps a little hard on him: 'Old Eli comes into view as a fat old man with about as much sense of God and care for people as a rhinoceros.'

WICKED PRIESTS

However, what really interests us about Eli are his two sons, Hophni and Phinehas, and his relationship with them. Eugene Peterson describes them as 'drunks with the sexual morals of tomcats'. They, too, were priests at Shiloh, but there was certainly little to admire about them. When we are introduced to them we are bluntly told that the sons of Eli were wicked men; they 'had no regard for the LORD' (1 Sam. 2:12). As the catalogue of their wickedness unfolds we are staggered at their arrogance and hypocrisy. They helped themselves to the best of the animals brought by the worshippers to sacrifice on God's altar. According to the record, 'The sin of the young men was very great in the LORD's sight, for they were treating the LORD's offering with contempt' (2:17). They also treated the women who served the Tent of the Meeting as sexual playmates. They had no redeeming features whatsoever.

There was no tabloid press in those days to publicize the young priests' behaviour 'in the public interest'. There was no need. It was public knowledge. Their behaviour and their brazen arrogance were talked about throughout the land. It certainly reached their father, Eli. 'I hear from all the people about these wicked deeds of yours. No, my sons; it is not a good report that I hear spreading among the LORD's people' (2:23–24). At least Eli spoke to them about their behaviour. Little good did it do.

A few years ago, a lady had occasion to rebuke

her three-year-old granddaughter. When the daughter asked the child what Granny had said, she replied, 'Blah, blah, blah!' So much for the rebuke or, rather, for the seriousness with which it was received! Likewise, Eli's sons simply shrugged their shoulders and continued with their offensive and godless lifestyle. 'His sons … did not listen to their father's rebuke, for it was the LORD's will to put them to death' (2:25).

Our essential focus, however, is on Eli, the elderly father.

In the early days of Israel, parents had a strong pastoral responsibility for the spiritual and moral upbringing and conduct of their children. The book of Deuteronomy has numerous references to that responsibility. Parents had to teach their children the ways of God (Deut. 4:9) and impress upon them God's commandments (6:7). The ways and requirements of God had to be part of the household conversation (11:19). Even the children of the non-Israelites who lived among them as 'aliens' had to be taught the law of God (31:12).

Eli must have been aware of that responsibility towards his two sons. Had he failed? Perhaps not entirely, for they had, after all, become priests, and must have known something of God's requirements even though they had come to treat them with contempt.

ELI'S FAILURE

Where Eli clearly failed was in his inaction. Whether out of misplaced fatherly love or sinful weakness, his response was to do nothing. When he remonstrated with them it was all just words. Similar situations are commonplace today. A parent rebukes a child in public for some form of undesirable behaviour. One rebuke follows another. Even threats follow. The bad behaviour continues. Yet the parent fails to act. Nothing changes. The onlookers take notice, as they did in the days of Eli and his sons. A new slant opens up on the famous saying attributed to Edmund Burke: 'All that is necessary for the triumph of evil is that good men do nothing.'

Eli must have lived with his failure for the rest of his life. Not for him an old age quietly giving thanks for the way his sons had turned out. Did he live these years wishing he had taken a stronger stand

and had acted in some decisive way to stop the rot?
Did his conscience rob these last years of the peace
which he ought to have known? Sadly, Eli suffered
part of the judgement which eventually fell on his
sons. When he heard of their deaths, along with the
capture of the ark of the covenant, 'Eli fell
backwards off his chair by the side of the gate. His
neck was broken and he died, for he was an old man
and heavy. He had led Israel for forty years' (1 Sam.
4:18).

This is a sad story, but one that is repeated, in
many of its aspects, time after time.

Given the inherent moral and spiritual weakness
of human beings (something which theologians
have called 'original sin'), it is reasonable to believe
that the story of Eli and his two sons has been
multiplied down through the centuries. A careful
search through the biographies in any decent
library would uncover illustrations of men or
women whose ways of life incurred the rebuke of
parents who themselves ultimately failed to act
decisively. The failure could have been due to lack
of courage, moral weakness, an easy-going
temperament or their own compromising way of

life. In his commentary on 2 Kings, Dale Ralph
Davis cites an interesting story which has some
similarities to that of Eli and his sons. Joseph P.
Kennedy was the father of some very prominent
figures in American history. One of his daughters
had a severe drinking problem. Five of his
grandchildren had a drug problem, one dying as a
result. Two grandchildren were alcoholics. One
was acquitted on a charge of rape, but was found
guilty of assault and battery. Dale Ralph Davis
concludes his story with these words: 'One cannot
negate personal responsibility, but at the same time
one cannot help but wonder if much of this is not
the fruit of the hard, driving and immoral Joe
Kennedy. A legacy is a frightening thing.'[1]

A young couple, both professing Christians,
refuse to insist that their children attend church
with them in the early days. 'We must allow them
absolute freedom of choice. The decision is theirs.'
Others watch the steady drift of the children away
from interest in Christian things, and feel sad at the
failure of the parents to make any attempt to resist
the invariable trend. If there have been words of
warning from the parents, they have been strangely

muted. The freedom of the children is being respected and the broadmindedness and tolerance of the parents are lauded by liberal friends, but others can only see the damage done, a damage fully seen in later life.

PARENTAL RESPONSIBILITY

The lessons from Eli's situation are all too obvious but have to be relearned in every generation. Parents dare not abrogate their responsibility to bring up their children in the way that they should go. It is the plain command of Scripture, after all. If sin is an offence to a holy God—and undoubtedly it is—it is to be rebuked in all its forms when it is seen in our offspring. If sin leads to death, as it did with Eli's sons, then every attempt must be made to correct or inhibit the sin and turn away the sinner from his or her ways. Lack of action is not an option in the older generation if we follow a holy God. Even grandparents, naturally afraid of interfering and giving the impression that they know best, must have some responsibility, difficult though it may be.

We began by saying that in our senior years we

tend to be more easy-going and tolerant. In some respects, that is admirable. Gone are the impulses to condemn and judge, occasionally with unlovely censoriousness. At other times, it is most certainly wrong. Age should not blunt our awareness of the damaging effects of a sinful and godless lifestyle. If we have the right to warn, rebuke or even stop what is happening, we should do so. The moral standards of societies may change, but God's are unchanging and clear. Judgement may not be the 'in' topic of many pulpits today, but it will continue to be God's provision for all who flout his will and law. Eli reminds us that judgement could well be uncomfortable for those who could have acted but did nothing.

Note

1 **Dale Ralph Davis,** *2 Kings: The Power and the Fury* (Focus on the Bible; Fearn: Christian Focus, 2005), p. 262.

5 Spirituality and old age

Psalm 71

O ne of the first books I ever read on the Psalms was *God in Man's Experience* by Leonard Griffith. I remember reading his words, 'The Psalms have meaning for us because they begin where we are. They find us in our human situation and they show us what happens when we bring the light of God to bear on our human situation … Every man can find himself somewhere in the book of Psalms.'

With the onset of old age, was I justified, on the basis of these words, to look for help in the Psalms? Imagine my delight on looking through a commentary to find Psalm 71 described as 'a psalm of old age'! Just the thing for my situation in my seventies!

Now, Psalm 71 itself has no heading, but the commentator's designation fits, as we shall see. The identity of the author is a mystery, but he was obviously not in the first flush of youth. We can tell this for he writes against the background of failing powers and even certain fears for old age. 'Do not cast me away when I am old; do not forsake me when my strength is gone' (v. 9). 'Even when I am old and grey, do not forsake me, O God' (v. 18).

Was he reflecting the fear of an older person finding him- or herself in a young person's world? Did he feel left behind by developments and changes? Did he feel cast aside, no longer 'with it'? These are not uncommon fears among older people—perhaps even greater in our rapidly developing world than in the world of the psalmist.

One commentator even goes so far as to claim that the disjointed nature of the psalm points to evidence of the ageing process in the author! According to him, the psalm is evidence of a sequence of 'senior moments' as the author skips from one thought to another and back again. If that claim is true, most of us older folk can sympathize!

DECKHANDS

It is easy, then, for those of us who are 'pensioners' to identify with this psalmist. Many of us feel, after active, involved and busy lives, that we have now turned into bystanders and spectators. Alan Redpath, once a prominent preacher, author and Christian leader, was once asked, 'What does it feel like to be retired?' He replied, 'Where once I was the skipper, now I'm learning to be a deckhand!' At least he had a certain continued involvement, for deckhands are useful, but many a person lacks even that in later years, and it sometimes hurts. We are no longer where the action is. Our resources to cope with a changing context are beginning to wane, if we ever really had them. Life, with its rapid changes, is leaving us behind and we experience a strange anxiety.

When I graduated in the early 1950s, the presiding academic read one of his own poems, which sums up the situation perfectly. It is the story of the elderly cat:

He blinks upon the hearth-rug,
And yawns in deep content,
Accepting all the comforts
That providence has sent.

OLD, BUT NOT OUT!

Louder he purrs, and louder
In one glad hymn of praise
For all the night's adventures,
For quiet, restful days.

Life will go on for ever,
With all that cat can wish;
Warmth and the glad procession
Of fish and milk and fish.

Only—the thought disturbs him—
He's noticed once or twice,
The times are somehow breeding
A nimbler race of mice.

(Alexander Gray, 'On a Cat, Ageing')

Fears can come in disturbing forms. Often we are surprised by the doubts which begin to form in our minds. We find ourselves asking, 'Was the stand I took worth it?', 'Am I as certain now as I once was?', 'What about the hereafter?' Rob Marchant, in *Pioneering the Third Age*, expresses it thus: 'The knowing that characterizes the second half of life is open to mystery, drawn to the depths and ready to

OLD, BUT NOT OUT!

risk … it is the time we begin to ask ourselves: What do I really know? What matters? What is the rock bottom of my faith?'

Our spirituality has to be considered in old age against the background of uncertainty and many of the subtle forms it takes.

ENEMIES

The psalmist was also conscious that he had enemies. His language in verses 10 and 11 is strong. These were people who were determined to do him in, who dismissed him and his faith. 'For my enemies speak against me; those who wait to kill me conspire together. They say, "God has forsaken him; pursue him and seize him, for no-one will rescue him."'

Our 'enemies' take, perhaps, a radically different form and few would accuse them of plotting our demise. Nevertheless, they are real. Not everyone is kindly disposed towards those who are older and appear, at times, anxious to put a break on progress and development. Not everyone welcomes comments on 'what used to happen' and constant comparisons with the past. Ian Knox, in *Older*

People and the Church, quotes a Church of England vicar as saying, 'The old—I feel frustrated by them: those who wish for a "golden age" which never was … They think that the Family Service is "irreverent", "entertainment". I resent their refusal to see things differently.'[1] We may speak of the decay of standards which once were meaningful to us, and this is interpreted as having a critical spirit and harking after 'the good old days'. They never really existed anyway!

Rob Marchant comes at the problem from a slightly different angle: '… in many ways the eyes and heart of the church have been seduced by the allure of youth. It fails to acknowledge the beauty of age, and for that there is a price to be paid.'[2] In too many of our churches the balance of effort is almost completely tipped in favour of youth work and comparatively little is done for the older generation. It takes little imagination to sense the reaction of an older, more experienced, mature Christian when told, 'You are the church of yesterday. We must concentrate on the young people—they are the church of tomorrow.' The pages of Christian periodicals have dozens of adverts for youth workers, and that is good, given the undoubted needs and opportunities. Absent, however, are adverts for specialist workers among older people, and yet we are told that the average age in the UK is getting higher. The spirituality of old age has its context in an environment of conceived redundancy and that is always a threat, if not an enemy, whatever our age.

SOURCES OF STRENGTH

The psalmist, in his old age, was aware of his personal fears and the threats from outside. Yet he was also aware of the sources of his strength.

There were the habits of a lifetime. 'Be my rock of refuge, to which I can always go' (v. 3). Some translations use 'continually' rather than 'always'. Similarly, verse 14 could read, 'But as for me, I shall continually have hope; I will praise you more and more.' In other words, the psalmist's strength lay in a developed habit of prayer, of laying all his circumstances before the God he had learned to trust. When fears and threats confronted him, it was his habit, developed over the years, to turn instantly to God. That was the way he had coped in the past and he saw no reason to break an engrained habit now. One writer puts it this way: 'You take into retirement the person your working years have formed. You prepare for old age by taking a positive attitude throughout your life and by living each stage fully.'

Old age gives us the opportunity to develop and enlarge that habit and, furthermore, to range far and wide with our prayers. We have time, now, to read the missionary magazines, to work through prayer bulletins and to respond to prayer requests—in other words, to develop our habit of prayer. The new frustrations and weaknesses which have come with the years are laid before the God we trust. The form they have taken over the years may have changed, but the God we address has not.

LOOKING BACK

Understandably, the psalmist also found his strength in his rich experience of God.

For you have been my hope,
    O Sovereign LORD,
my confidence since my youth.
From my birth I have relied on you;

OLD, BUT NOT OUT!

you brought me forth from my mother's womb.

I will ever praise you ...

Though you have made me see troubles, many and bitter,

you will restore my life again;

from the depths of the earth

you will bring me up.

You will increase my honour

and comfort me once again. (vv. 5–6, 20–21)

What a remarkable testimony and an immense trust he displayed! In his weakness and frailty he ranged up and down his past. Everywhere in his life he detected the faithfulness and goodness of God. When doubts and enemies were pitted against him, he simply pondered the evidence of the past and was at peace.

When all Thy mercies, O my God

My rising soul surveys,

Transported with the view, I'm lost

In wonder, love and praise. (Joseph Addison, 1712)

The spirituality of old age has a backwards look to it that detects and rejoices in God's faithfulness

OLD, BUT NOT OUT!

over the years. Even as we recollect dark periods we can now, from our older vantage point, see God's gracious hand and provision.

Perhaps it would be good for us, in the later years of our lives, to read some books on church history. They are not usually dry tomes of uninteresting facts and figures. They are records, certainly, of the follies and mistakes of the church over the years, but they are also records of the intervention of a faithful God and the remarkable people he raised up to challenge the times in which they lived. These records are a reminder that God has not gone to sleep, that what he has done in the past he will continue to do in the future, and that he is not frustrated by the problems of any age.

A ROBUST HOPE

We are told that when hope dies, we are finished. This psalmist is not finished by a long chalk! He possesses a robust hope and so, not surprisingly, he is strong. 'Though you have made me see troubles, many and bitter, you will restore my life again; from the depths of the earth you will again bring me up. You will increase my honour and comfort me once again' (vv. 20–21). Strictly speaking, the psalmist has no sense of an ultimate resurrection, but he is strengthened by a resolute hope that weakness, frailty and the efforts of his enemies do not have the last word.

What we can take from this is that without hope, the future for all of us is nothing but gradual deterioration of our mental and physical powers, leading ultimately to death. By contrast, for the person of faith, the best is yet to be. It is possible, when we pass into our senior years, to talk of 'the good old days' as if the future will be inferior, if not second-best. The spirituality of old age for the Christian, however, is not that of regret, but of anticipation, hope, promise and renewal. 'So we fix our eyes not on what is seen, but on what is unseen. For what is seen is temporary, but what is unseen is eternal' (2 Cor. 4:18).

SHARING GOD'S FAITHFULNESS

One further feature of this 'psalm of old age' is worth mentioning. The writer had a burning urge to speak. He could not restrain himself from telling of God's goodness, righteousness and salvation.

OLD, BUT NOT OUT!

From verse 15 and then again from verse 22 he writes of his intention to be resolute in testifying to all that God means to him.

It has to be admitted that the pressure on us as we grow older is to keep quiet more often. It was said of one older friend that 'He had yesterday's answers to today's questions', and that charge is enough to silence anyone. There is a great deal of validity in the following prayer,

Lord, Thou knowest better than I know myself that I am growing older, and will someday be old. Keep me from … the fatal habit of thinking that I must say something on every subject and on every occasion. Release me from craving to try to straighten out everybody's affairs. Keep my mind free from the recital of endless details—give me wings to get to the point … With my vast store of wisdom, it seems a pity not to use it all—but Thou knowest, Lord, that I want a few friends at the end.[3]

The psalmist wasn't a garrulous old bore. Rather, he was a man brimful of the Lord's goodness and he couldn't help speaking about it. What could conceivably be wrong with that?

Would that more of us, with a lifetime's experience of God's faithfulness and with hope brimming in our hearts, felt the same urge to share and testify!

Notes

1 **Ian S. Knox,** *Older People and the Church* (London/New York: T & T Clark, 2002), p. 120.

2 **Rob Marchant,** *Pioneering the Third Age: The Church in an Ageing Population* (Carlisle: Paternoster, 2003).

3 Author unknown.

6 The contentment of old age

Psalm 131

fter he retired, my father suffered a stroke. He seemed at first to recover from its debilitating effects but, gradually, he lost his ability to move and even to communicate. At times there were tears, the tears of frustration at not being able to relate to those who loved him. When eventually he died, we discovered his Bible bookmark at Psalm 131. We liked to think that, in the bewilderment of his incapacity, he found peace and contentment in what the psalmist expresses there. It is certainly a psalm for those whose minds are battered by questions and who are at risk of frustration and confusion.

It was Spurgeon who said of this psalm, 'It is one of the shortest Psalms to read, but one of the longest to learn.'[1] So much that happens to us in life seems puzzling and confusing, and to lack meaning and explanation. It almost seems natural to demand answers to the many questions which varied experiences pose and to find a reason for every happening, especially the disasters which come to us all: 'Why has this happened to me?' 'What is the purpose of this experience?' It is not unknown for well-meaning Christians to ask friends passing through a difficult time, 'Have you thought of what God is saying to you in this?'

The psalmist appears to turn his back on such questioning and demands. The title says that this psalm was written by David, and he was no stranger to the whole range of life's experiences. He had good reason to question and demand. Yet, in this psalm, he refuses to do so.

A FRETFUL CHILD

The psalmist writes as a thoroughly contented man, the opposite of the person who, in his 'haughtiness' and 'pride' (see v. 1), feels he has the right to know, understand and have the reason for everything revealed to him. He is quite prepared to accept that there are questions he cannot answer and events he cannot fully understand. He will not be like a fretful baby denied its mother's milk, crying in frustration and fury.

We live in a world where 'rights' are all-important and freedom of information is enshrined in legislation. It is not surprising that we find ourselves saying, 'I have a right to know what is hidden,' and 'I have a right to know the explanation for what is puzzling about my experiences.' We can have a certain sympathy for Job's friends who, in effect, were saying to Job, 'There must be a reason for your condition. Why don't you demand it—seek it out?' For David, that is the path of 'haughtiness' and 'pride' and he will have none of it. The apostle Paul mirrored the same attitude: 'I have learned the secret of being content in any and every situation' (Phil. 4:12). For many of us, that is difficult. We may even be afraid that contentment is just another word for resignation, and we sense that that has no place in the Christian life.

Dwell for a moment on this haughtiness and pride. Is it not sinful presumption to demand to see the end from the beginning and to understand, with Godlike clarity, every experience of life? There are some Christians who give the impression that every action of God is complicated and involved, demanding from us special insight and unique gifts of understanding. The plots of the early spy novels of John le Carré were full of bluff and counter-bluff, coded signals, false trails, twists and turns. Nothing was quite what it appeared to be on the surface. Is that the way God acts? Does he deliberately play with us so that his dealings with us require special skills of deduction? A student made heavy weather of his time at university. He sincerely believed that every exam question was a trick question and meant something other than it plainly said. He therefore needed to fathom what the examiner was really after. Not surprisingly, he failed examination after examination!

To make his point, David uses a lovely illustration which most parents will appreciate: 'But I have stilled and quietened my soul; like a weaned child with its mother, like a weaned child is my soul within me' (v. 2). There was a point in his life when, if he didn't have an explanation, he reacted a bit like an infant denied its mother's milk. His hunger for an answer had to be instantly satisfied or he made his feelings known! Now, however, he was like a weaned child. His new attitude was a transition from infantile, insecure bolshiness to something better and more mature. He had come to believe that, when we are faced with life's mysteries, God calls for not the proud determination of the interrogator, but the trust of a weaned child.

A NEW TRUST

In other words, the psalmist had learned trust rather than insecurity. The infant baby senses its vulnerability, while the maturing child has (hopefully!) learned to trust the adult caring for it. Our relationship to our God is to be not that of fearful infants, but of robust people who know God's track record. Fretfulness marks the inexperience of youth, while trust is a sign of maturity.

Job expressed that trust even as his friends pressed him to find clear answers. 'Though he slay me, yet will I hope in him' (Job 13:15). Our Lord was also content to leave matters in his Father's hands: 'Yet not as I will, but as you will' (Matt. 26:39b).

Mrs Charles E. Cowman and her husband served the church in Asia for over twenty years until her husband's health failed. She compiled the book *Streams in the Desert*, which includes some lines summing the matter up:

I cannot know why suddenly the storm

Should rage around me in its wrath:

But this I know.

God watches all my path

And I can trust.

I have no power to look across the tide

To see while here the land beyond the river;

But this I know—I shall be God's forever;

So I can trust.[2]

David had also learned confidence rather than fear. Like a squealing baby, we are often afraid that God will not be there when we need him or will withdraw what is necessary for Christian living. God requires from us, however, not the fear of the infant but the confidence of childlikeness. That confidence tells us that the unseen God will supply every need—indeed, knows these needs even before we articulate them—and is committed to blessing us. A grandchild approaching her teens and who had been quite prepared, as a baby, to make a noise when her feed was even slightly late, expressed that maturing confidence in these words: 'I know that God created me, and I know that my parents wanted me and love me.' That confidence is a glorious thing in a world where so many live in the fear of unanswered questions and uncertainty.

ASSURANCE

In the psalm, David's words express assurance rather than insecurity. The baby finds security in the warm, felt, physical contact with the mother. The immature Christian needs the security of the seen, the visible and the felt, whether it be a building, ritual, symbol, vivid experience or sign. Without something that can be felt or experienced, there is a sense of unmet need, and we cry out in fear.

God, however, longs for us to have the assurance that he will give us our 'daily bread' and that he is here with us, real, though unseen and often unfelt.

It is sad when we are still caught up in the

mother's-milk syndrome. Unless we can feel, see or experience, we indulge in the equivalent of crying. Such an attitude is a sign of not having fully grown up. Was that the situation addressed in the epistle to the Hebrews? 'You need milk, not solid food! Anyone who lives on milk, being still an infant, is not acquainted with the teaching about righteousness. But solid food is for the mature …' (Heb. 5:12–14a).

It has to be admitted that many Christians find the transition from spiritual infancy difficult. It is often easier to be querulous infants than trusting adults. The time of weaning is often noisy and our crying takes the form of innumerable questions. 'Why do I not have the vivid experiences I once had? Have I lost something vital?' The answer has to be 'No! You are now living by faith and not by sight! You have been weaned away from the visible, the felt.'

As we get older, such a reminder is important. Many of the factors which once seemed part and parcel of our discipleship have either disappeared or have changed out of all recognition. We depended on the unchanging nature of the worship service on a Sunday. We knew what came next in the hymn/prayer sandwich and it gave us a certain sense of security when the world outside was changing fast. Now the sandwich is out of fashion and anything can happen in the service. The menu changes every week. The very building, which was so dear to us and encouraged our sense of worship, has had its pews taken out or has been replaced by a borrowed school hall which seems so bare. Or maybe—even worse—our church has united with another, and we use 'their' building and not 'ours'. The godly leaders, venerable to our youthful eyes and so smart in their dress, have given way to cheery 'worship leaders' with a disquieting and upsetting informality in their language and clothing. What one Christian leader called 'the beat of the times' has replaced 'the cadences of eternity'. Silence is out and noise is in. It takes a robust and mature faith to trust and feel secure amid the changes we experience, even in church life today. The psalmist points the way. We ought to have moved beyond our infant-like dependencies and know that we are securely bound to the very origin of all we need—an unchanging God who is the

OLD, BUT NOT OUT!

source of complete *contentment* and satisfaction. Is that not a great comfort to Christians who have been on the road for some time?

The psalmist's final word is very relevant as the years advance and bewildering and unsettling experiences hit us: 'put your hope in the LORD both now and for evermore' (v. 3). It simply sums up what the psalm has been saying to us, especially to those of us advanced in years. 'Don't be a baby! That's the way of demanded answers, dependence on the externals and self-centredness.' Childlikeness is the way of trust, confidence and assurance. 'I tell you the truth, unless you change and become like little children ...' (Matt. 18:3).

Father, I place into your hands
the things that I can't do.
Father, I place into your hands
the times that I've been through.
Father I place into your hands
the way that I should go,
for I know I always can trust you.

(Jenny Hewer © 1975 Thankyou Music)

OLD, BUT NOT OUT!

Notes

1 **C. H. Spurgeon,** 'Psalm 131: Title', *The Treasury of David*; accessed at www.biblestudytools.com, August 2012.

2 **L. B. Cowman,** *Streams in the Desert: 366 Devotional Readings*, ed. James Reimann (Grand Rapids, MI: Zondervan, 1997), p. 196.

7 The discernment of old age

Luke 2:21–40

I f Simeon and Anna had lived in our day and generation we would have considered them 'past it' because of their age. The high spots of their lives must have been long gone and old age offered nothing but decline and memories. Yet it was not so—emphatically not! As they got older, 'the best was yet to be'! They are a reminder that, even in our later years, there can be moments of enlightenment and inspiration, spiritual highs which are the climax of long years of faithfulness and commitment. How many of us have met their modern counterparts—people often long past their supposed prime but whose spiritual perception and understanding are profound and inspiring.

We know nothing about Simeon and Anna's backgrounds, yet their story has immense significance. They were, of course, old. We presume that of Simeon, but with Anna we know it to be true. Luke 2:36–37 could read, 'she had been married for only seven years and had been a widow for eighty-four years'. Since in those days girls got married at about the age of twelve, simple mathematics suggest that she could have been over a hundred! She was an old woman by any standard.

So, an old couple were among the first to recognize the infant Jesus as the Messiah. Dismiss the spiritual insight of the elderly at your peril!

A NEW REVOLUTION

Another fact, obvious when stated but capable of being missed, is that the Messiah, even in his infant state, was recognized by both a man and a woman. In a culture in which women lacked the status of men (to say the least), Anna's confession was the shape of the revolution to come. Women were to play a significant part in our Lord's later ministry and in the history of the young church. Was Anna, old as she was, a pointer to the future, when women, in increasing numbers, were to recognize the Christ and acknowledge him as Lord? Men, then or now, have no monopoly on spiritual discernment.

The encounters of Simeon and Anna with the infant Jesus came at a significant moment. Mary and Joseph were obeying the Jewish law which required that a woman, forty days after giving birth, should go to the temple and offer a sacrifice for purification. She could offer a lamb for a burnt offering and a pigeon or dove for a sin offering. If she was facing financial hardship she could offer 'a pair of doves or two young pigeons' (Luke 2:24; see Lev. 12:8). Mary and Joseph were obviously in the latter situation. Yet, despite their poverty, their obedience made it a highly significant event for them.

In addition, it was also the *redemption* of Mary's firstborn son (Luke 2:23). She was obeying the commands of Exodus 13: 'Consecrate to me every firstborn male. The first offspring of every womb among the Israelites belongs to me, whether man or animal' (v. 2); 'you are to give over to the LORD the first offspring of every womb … Redeem every firstborn among your sons' (12a, 13b). So the infant Jesus was being 'bought back'.

On all counts, therefore, the visit of Mary and Joseph with the infant Jesus to the temple was a deeply spiritual occasion. It was to become even more so when they met Simeon and Anna.

Simeon was the first person they met. Even a superficial reading of the encounter removes all thought that he was an ageing soul with a tired mind and fading spirituality. There is much to commend him in the account. Indeed, would that we had more like him among the elderly!

He was 'righteous and devout' (Luke 2:25). 'Righteous' indicates that he behaved well towards others. 'Devout' describes his relationship towards God. Years later, when standing before Felix, the apostle Paul was to claim that he had tried to live in the same way: 'So I strive always to keep my conscience clear before God and man' (Acts 26:16).

So this was a good and godly man. Is there not a suggestion here that such a man, or woman for that matter, because of his or her consistent godliness, possesses a special sensitivity to what God is doing? Paul was later to suggest that when we are 'transformed by the renewing of [our] mind' we shall 'be able to test and approve what God's will is—his good, pleasing and perfect will' (Rom. 12:2). If Simeon's faith had been casual and his standing poor among his contemporaries, do you think his perception in spiritual matters would have been quite so acute?

A SUSTAINING HOPE

Simeon also had a sustaining hope: 'He was waiting for the consolation of Israel, and the Holy Spirit was upon him. It had been revealed to him by the Holy Spirit that he would not die before he had seen the Lord's Christ' (2:25–26). He lived by the hope, inspired by the Holy Spirit of God, that he would see the Messiah—the fulfilment of God's promise to his people. We can imagine the pressures on him, especially as the years passed and nothing happened, to give up his hope and doubt the promise. Yet this elderly man maintained his hope. It wasn't an empty, foundationless optimism, but a hope based on a promise of God. There's a mighty difference!

Not all elderly people know what hope means. J. I. Packer eloquently describes the plight of many older people in *A Passion for Holiness*:

One of the saddest things today is the number of elderly people who, not being believers, have nothing to look forward to. Their life is fading away. Their bodies are getting feeble and breaking down. They cannot do what they used to do, and will never be able to do it again. They feel that they are moving deeper and deeper into a dark cave, with the darkness thickening around them, and no light, or way out, for them at the end. They find living without hope to be an unrelieved burden. They get bitter in heart, and sunk in self-pity and nostalgia. If they become (as, alas, they sometimes do) a misery to others, it is because they first became in this way a misery to themselves. Hopelessness wastes the spirit.[1]

Ask many of our contemporaries what hope sustains their lives, especially in their later years, and if you get an answer at all, it could well be in terms of winning the lottery! J. B. Priestly, in his autobiography, *Instead of the Trees*, speaks for many when he confesses, 'I hate being old … In old age we are compelled to play a bad character part not belonging to our essential and enduring self … we no longer have anything important to contribute.' He also speaks of a suicide note left by an old person: 'So tired of buttoning and unbuttoning.' It is the routine of the monotonous.

OLD, BUT NOT OUT!

Tomorrow will be the same as today. Hope is missing from their vocabulary.

What a contrast we see in Simeon's life and attitude! Though so much in us is undoubtedly fading and wearing out, he calls us to have a strong and resolute hope in the promises of God. It means that, as we grow older, we have a hope of a growing personal experience of God's grace and love, a hope of renewal and revival within his church, a hope of seeing the nations won for Christ, a hope of a glorious inheritance and, above all, a hope of the return of our Lord and Saviour. The Holy Spirit will be the source and inspiration of that multi-faceted hope. By God's grace, we can all live as Simeon lived, nourishing our hope on the promises of God. What meaning that will give to life!

THE HOLY SPIRIT

Simeon was also a man who knew the reality of the Holy Spirit. Three times we have a reference to the Spirit of God in relationship to his life. What is interesting is how the Spirit manifested himself in Simeon's life. Two words sum it up: sensitivity and discernment. He was sensitive to what the Spirit had to say about the coming of the Messiah, and when he saw the child Jesus he was able to recognize him by the discernment of the Spirit. Others saw only a poor couple and their baby. Simeon saw God's salvation incarnate and the implications that would follow his coming into the world.

The late Archbishop Donald Coggan, in a sermon at the 1978 Lambeth Conference of Anglican Bishops, described a bishop as 'one who is open to the wind of the Spirit, warmed by the fire of the Spirit, on the look-out for the surprises of the Spirit'. Why limit that definition to bishops? In a real sense, all that was true of Simeon. Is it unreasonable to suggest that, the older we grow and the more our openness to Scripture develops, the greater will be our sensitivity to what the Holy Spirit is saying to us and, through us, to others?

Mark Greene of the London Institute for Contemporary Christianity made a perceptive comment about Simeon in his Christmas letter of 2009:

... for Simeon, this forty-day-old baby in the temple courts was wonder enough ...

OLD, BUT NOT OUT!

Enough. Not just for that moment, or that day, or that week, but enough to go to his death replete with contentment, brimming with joy that what God had promised him was here before his very eyes. Indeed the Messiah, in swaddling clothes, so overwhelmed every natural instinct to prolong his own physical life that Simeon could say to God: 'You may now dismiss your servant in peace' (Luke 2:29).

But it was only a baby.

For Simeon, the baby was a guarantee of things to come, a pinprick of light absolutely guaranteeing a new dawn. The God who had begun something would finish it.

So, for Simeon, contentment was mixed in with hope. Hope had sustained him throughout the years of waiting, but he saw it realized and fulfilled as he looked at the Messiah, albeit as a baby. Now his hope was replaced with a deep contentment. God had fulfilled his promises. The Messiah had come. Light had entered the darkness. No longer was there the possibility that things would go wrong in God's redeeming plan. The end point of God's purposes had begun.

OLD, BUT NOT OUT!

In a strange way, we can enter into Simeon's contentment. As the years advance, it is so easy to be overwhelmed by the darkness and wrong around us. Sometimes it can seem as if the world is descending fast into the abyss. Yet the Christian who has recognized the Messiah in Jesus of Nazareth is content that God's answer has become incarnate. The process of 'making all things new' has become visible. Anxiety and pessimism no longer rule. We can be content as we realize that God is at work and his kingdom has assuredly come, and is coming.

AN OLD LADY

Then there was Anna. She was, as we have seen, a widow of long standing. No doubt life was hard. There was no widows' pension or social security payment to ease the struggle. Yet, for her, there was no sitting back moping in a corner of her home. She had developed the habit of frequenting the temple, where she gave herself to fasting and prayer. Her heightened spiritual sensitivity and her undoubted love for God and for worshipping him led not merely to recognition, but also to a compulsion to tell of that discovery with all who shared her anticipation of the Messiah and the liberation he would bring. Luke tells us that 'she spoke about the child to all who were looking forward to the redemption of Jerusalem' (2:38). The tense used here adds meaning to her actions: 'she kept speaking'. Anna could be a role model for all ages!

How do widows, or widowers for that matter, spend their time, and what occupies their thoughts? The temptation must be strong, and natural, to dwell on the past. Everything good and hoped for in younger years is now largely history and the future yawns ahead in bleak emptiness. There is sometimes a brittleness and a sadness about them which communicates itself to others. That may be a generalization, but it is sadly true in many cases.

Here, however, in Anna, we find a woman walking closely with her God, disciplined in her devotions, and for whom the future and God's fulfilment of his promise meant everything. Her last years were her best. They would be years of thankfulness and contentment. The same can be true of the physically old today, as they develop a

OLD, BUT NOT OUT!

deeper understanding of the purposes of God and their glorious fulfilment in Jesus Christ.

Note

1 **J. I. Packer,** *A Passion for Holiness* (Cambridge: Crossway, 1992), p. 247.

8 The anticipation of old age

2 Timothy 4:6–8

A visit to St Paul's Cathedral in London is always inspiring and moving. Who can fail to be impressed by that mighty building, its dome and its dominance of the skyline? Within the cathedral there are many interesting things to see, among them a copy of William Holman Hunt's painting *The Light of the World*, depicting our Lord standing at the door and knocking. One of the most fascinating, however, can easily be missed. Down behind the choir stalls, hanging on the wall, is a framed page from an exercise book. It is a letter dated 27 July 1942 and written 'Somewhere in the Papuan Bush'. This is the last letter penned by the Anglican missionary and priest Vivian Redlich a few days before his martyrdom at the hands of a local tribe. It reads,

My Dear Dad, The war has busted up here. I got back from Doguara and ran right into it—am now somewhere in my parish trying to carry on, tho' my people are horribly scared. No news of May and I am cut off from contacting her—my staff OK so far but in another spot. I'm trying to stick it whatever happens. If I don't come out of it just rest content that I have tried to do my job faithfully. Last chance of getting word out: so forgive brevity. God bless you all. Vivian

It is difficult to read that without being profoundly moved. Years after I first saw it, I mentioned it to an Anglican clergyman. He had just told me that he had recently returned from Papua. It turned out that he had been attending the inauguration of a new bishop there who had been led into the Christian ministry by the challenge of that letter. I did not find it difficult to believe.

The apostle Paul was in an almost similar situation to that of Vivian Redlich. He gave expression of it as he wrote to young Timothy,

For I am already being poured out like a drink offering, and the time has come for my departure. I have fought the good fight, I have finished the race, I have kept the faith. Now there is in store for me the crown of righteousness, which the Lord, the righteous Judge, will award to me on that day—and not

OLD, BUT NOT OUT!

only to me, but also to all who have longed for his appearing.
(2 Tim. 4:6–8)

These two men, the apostle Paul and Vivian
Redlich, faced the imminent end of their lives here
on earth, probably both by violent means. Unless
we bury our heads very deeply in the sand, we all
know that we shall, unless the Lord first returns,
face the end of our mortal lives at some time in the
future. Thankfully, for most of us it will not come
by violent means—but it will come. In the light of
this, it is worth looking a little more closely at
Paul's testimony to his young disciple Timothy.

What is immediately striking is how unusual the
apostle's attitude is to his death compared with that
of most people. Paul Johnson, in *Modern Times*,
quotes Stalin's daughter's description of her
father's death: 'his last gesture being to lift his left
hand as if to curse, or to ward off something'. J. I.
Packer describes a report he received of a visit a
friend had paid to an old headmaster. 'How was
he?' asked Packer. 'Terribly gloomy,' came the
reply. 'I asked him what he was doing these days
and all he would say was "waiting for the end".'[1]

OLD, BUT NOT OUT!

Woody Allen, the actor and film producer, joked about the inevitable: 'I am not afraid of death, I just don't want to be there when it happens.'[2] In more serious mode, he wrote an article in *Esquire* in 1977 in which he said, 'The fundamental thing behind all motivation and all activity is the constant struggle against annihilation and against death. It's absolutely stupefying in its terror, and it renders anyone's accomplishments meaningless.'[3]

Are these feelings typical of many in our day and age? If so, they couldn't be more different from the attitude of Paul the apostle as he writes to Timothy.

A DRINK OFFERING

Paul sees death as a drink offering poured out before God. Indeed, he goes further than that and suggests, as the tense indicates, that this offering is in process even as he writes. This man, who has written elsewhere of the necessity for the Lord's disciples to offer themselves as 'living sacrifices' (Rom. 12:1), sees his own life, and impending death, as a libation poured out before God's altar. The reference is to the drink offering described in Numbers 15:1–12, 28; 7:22, the instructions for which contain the repeated phrase 'an aroma pleasing to the LORD'. Paul's use of this image was far from being the presumptuous boast of a proud man. He was acutely aware of being 'the chief of sinners', as he had already reminded Timothy (see 1 Tim. 1:15, NKJV), but he sensed that his life of obedience and commitment were pleasing to his Lord, and that his death and acceptance before God would be the climax of that pleasure.

That Christian is well blessed who, mindful of his or her debt to the unmerited grace of God, can sense God's pleasure with his or her life and anticipate God's delight at the end. 'Well done, good and faithful servant,' is the welcome we all long to hear as we enter God's eternal presence. Our death will be the final act of our drink offering, 'an aroma pleasing to the LORD'.

Paul also refers to his death as 'my departure'. The word picture in the original Greek is a vivid one. It suggests the unyoking of animals after a hard day's work in the fields, the striking of camp and, above all, the casting off of a ship before a voyage. So Paul is saying, 'The burden of my ministry is about to lift, the earthly tent I have lived in [see 2 Cor. 5:1] is about to be destroyed, the ropes are slipped and I'm about to set off for another shore!' Death, by whatever means, held no fears for him. He saw it as a release and new life. Earlier, he had expressed his longing for that experience: 'I desire to depart and be with Christ, which is better by far' (Phil. 1:23).

Again, the contrast between the Christian and the non-believer is striking. Barbara Wootton, a prominent member of the House of Lords some years back, concluded in her autobiographical *In a World I Never Made* that 'death is to be equated with the extinction of human consciousness and correctly defined as an irreversible coma'. That is certainly the view held by many who are strangers to, or opposed to, Christian truth and experience.

A GLORIOUS ARRIVAL

For the Christian following and loving Jesus Christ, it is otherwise. Our death may come slowly as the body declines; it may come as a result of some painful and distressing illness; it may come suddenly by some unforeseen accident; or it may come, as it did to the apostle, by martyrdom. By whatever means, it will be a departure followed by a glorious arrival. Donald Cargill, the Scottish Covenanter, suffered martyrdom in Edinburgh's Grassmarket on 27 July 1681. Before he was beheaded, the crowds heard him cry, 'Now for the morning and the King's face. No more night and no more darkness.'

Many a disciple of Christ, contemplating his or her probable 'departure', has regrets regarding the quality of past service. Most of us can look back on mistakes and shortcomings. 'If only I had seized the opportunities which presented themselves! If only I had approached things differently! If only I had done more!' All that is understandable. Yet the fact is that Paul looked at his years of missionary service with a degree of satisfaction. Not that it had been easy; the two images he employs when he writes to Timothy stress that.

THE GOOD FIGHT

Paul said that his life as a follower of Jesus had been like a 'good fight'. It had been like a stern conflict in a gladiatorial arena, but he had acquitted himself well. Sometimes the conflict had taken a very physical form, as he reminded the Corinthian church. He wrote that, while in Ephesus, he had 'fought wild beasts' (1 Cor. 15:32). Later, he wrote of being bombarded with various assaults: 'We are hard pressed on every side, but not crushed; perplexed, but not in despair; persecuted, but not abandoned; struck down, but not destroyed' (2 Cor. 4:8–9). It had truly been a battle, but he had done more than survive. He had been more than a conqueror (Rom. 8:37).

'For Believers Fighting' was a section title in the first Methodist hymn book. The Christian life involves conflict, often grim and unrelenting. We confront pressures which would squeeze the life out of us. We experience temptations which, were we to give in, would compromise our Christian integrity. We face attacks on our faith, sometimes insidious but at other times full frontal. It is not an easy life and much of the conflict is long-lasting and determined. Most of us in our later years could bear testimony to that. God grant that when life is nearing its end, despite our weaknesses and faltering moments, we are able to share something of the apostle's claim to have fought well.

A RACE

The second image Paul employs in these verses is that of a race. As he contemplated the end of his life on earth he was able to say, 'I have finished the race.' The significance of that claim came home to me when a half-marathon was being staged locally. The weather on the day was atrocious: a biting cold wind accompanied by frequent snow flurries. It was not a day to be outside, far less to run a half-marathon in! Yet the runners did it. It would have been no small achievement to finish the race that morning. Similarly, it had not been easy for Paul, and nor is it ever easy for those who are faithful to their calling in Christ Jesus. Samuel Rutherford wrote in 1637 to Mr Alexander Henderson, 'God has called you to Christ's side, and the wind is now in Christ's face in this land; and seeing ye are with Him, ye cannot expect the lee-side, or the sunny side of the brae [hill].'[4]

The Galatian Christians had been slowed up by weather conditions. 'You were running a good race,' wrote Paul. 'Who cut in on you and kept you from obeying the truth?' (Gal. 5:7). Most of us, looking back on our lives, would feel uncomfortable if faced with that question. Yet our call is to steady progress—persevering despite the alien pressures, whether they come from others, the society in which we live or elsewhere. We don't need to be sprinters, either. William Carey wrote to his nephew,

Eustace, if after my removal anyone should think it worth his while to write my Life, I will give you a criterion by which you may judge of its correctness. If he give me credit for being a plodder, he will describe me justly. Anything beyond this will be too much. I can plod. I can persevere in any definite pursuit. To this I owe everything.[5]

Surely Paul was not writing solely about those periods in his life when everything seemed to go smoothly and easily. He had in mind that steady, unremitting perseverance inspired by the call of God and the strength and endurance of the Holy Spirit. If we can look back on a life lived like that, we can come near to the end of it with a sense of joyous peace. Paul would have endorsed these words of Sir Francis Drake to one of his admirals in 1587—he was referring to warfare at sea but his words could also apply to the race of life: 'There must be a beginning of any great matter, but the continuing unto the end until it be thoroughly finished yields the true glory.'[6]

KEEPING THE FAITH

Paul also assured his young friend, 'I have kept the faith.' In other words, 'I have carefully kept the gospel message committed to my charge.' Already in this letter to Timothy he had likened the gospel to a deposit which had to be guarded and preserved: 'What you heard from me, keep as the pattern of sound teaching, with faith and love in Christ Jesus. Guard the good deposit that was entrusted to you—guard it with the help of the Holy Spirit who lives in us' (2 Tim. 1:13–14). Was he now saying to Timothy, 'Follow my example. The message entrusted to me has never been watered down, changed to accommodate my critics or altered in any way, despite innumerable pressures to do so'? The whole history of Paul's ministry bears witness to this claim.

In our postmodern society, we are constantly being told that we must change our approach, even our vocabulary, if we are to communicate the gospel. The pressure is strong, and often insidious, to change in some way the content or to soft-pedal its essential challenge. The result can so easily bear little resemblance to the 'offence of the cross' which was the kernel of the gospel that Paul guarded. We don't want to offend the outwardly respectable neighbour who is asking serious questions by speaking too boldly about her sinful condition before a holy God. We don't want to upset the friend who is proud of his religiosity by insisting that it isn't enough or that it's even mistaken. We don't want to be regarded as 'odd', so we try not to be too controversial in any stance we take. We don't want to be excluded from certain social circles, so we water down the reality of our faith. We can so easily end up with a half-gospel; but we are rebuked by some words from the Scottish theologian P. T. Forsyth: 'Half-gospels have no dignity and no future. Like the famous mule, they have neither pride of ancestry nor hope of posterity.'[7]

Despite pressures to compromise, to add or subtract from the truth of the gospel and to downplay inconvenient aspects of God's revealed Word, Paul was not ashamed to say that he 'kept the faith'. The call to such resolution and faithfulness has not diminished over the years. The pressures have not decreased, though they may have changed their form. The challenge to 'keep the faith' comes to all Christians, young and old.

CELEBRATING WITH OUR LORD

The end of life was drawing near for the apostle. Nero's verdict was a near certainty. Its painful consequences would have to be endured. What gripped Paul's mind, however, was that what lay beyond would be a magnificent reversal of the verdict of a Roman emperor. 'Now there is in store for me a crown of righteousness, which the Lord, the righteous Judge will award to me …' (2 Tim. 4:8). What also gladdened his heart was the conviction that he would share that crown with all 'who have longed for his appearing'. The past, for every faithful servant of Jesus Christ, has known temptation and pressure, hardship and suffering. At the end, there is the matter of physical death to be experienced—but the future is glorious. 'Well done, good and faithful servant! ... Come and share your master's happiness!' (Matt. 25:21).

Notes

1 **J. I. Packer,** *A Passion for Holiness* (Cambridge: Crossway, 1992), p. 247.

2 Quoted at BrainyQuote, www.brainyquote.com/; accessed August 2012.

3 Quoted at thegospelcoalition.org/blogs/rayortlund/2010/11/15/except-in-a-slapdash-way/; from **Frank Rich,** "Woody Allen Wipes the Smile off his Face," *Esquire*, May 1977, p. 75; accessed August 2012.

4 **Andrew Bonar,** (ed.), *Letters of Samuel Rutherford* (Edinburgh: Oliphant, Anderson and Ferrier, 1891).

5 **Eustace Carey,** *Memoir of William Carey, D.D.: Shoemaker and Missionary* (London: Jackson and Walford, 1836), p. vii.

6 Quoted on Wikiquote: en.wikiquote.org/wiki/Francis_Drake; accessed August 2012.

7 **Peter Taylor Forsyth,** *The Church and the Sacraments* (London: Independent Press, 1947), p. 18.

9 Old, but not out!

My wife and I once sat down and counted. Between us we knew at least half a dozen friends who were over ninety years of age. Delightfully, with perhaps one exception, they were fit, even sprightly. During a visit to a relative in the South of England, he introduced me to his golfing partner, who occasionally sat down on a portable seat between some quite excellent shots. 'How old are you?' I eventually dared to ask. 'Ninety-four,' was his brisk answer! As an added bonus, the people on our list were all committed Christians with a steady, lively faith enriched by their long years of experience.

Were we unusual in knowing so many in their nineties? The data suggests that our experience is normal. The Office of National Statistics tells us that there are currently over twelve million people over the age of sixty in the UK; that is a fifth of the population. In just five years, from 1983 to 1988, the number of British citizens reaching 100 years old rose from 1,250 to 1,710. It is estimated that the numbers of those over 100 years old will have increased from 300 in 1950 to 3,000 a century later.

So there is no doubt that we are an ageing population. The evidence is all around us. There are just more of us, whether we call ourselves oldies, old age pensioners, senior citizens, the chronologically enriched or, as one noticeboard described us, 'super adults'!

Naturally, the age situation is reflected in our churches—some would say, even more so. Some churches undoubtedly have a higher proportion of senior citizens in relation to younger age groups, although there are glorious exceptions. We have already touched on the high priority given to youth work compared with the relative failure to have much specialized work among the elderly, who are often in the majority. So the older age groups occasionally feel ignored—'taken for granted', or even 'put out to grass'—in their churches, particularly where there is a vibrant youth work. Those who talk of seniors as 'the church of yesterday' seldom reflect on what they are saying. Does that mean that they are no longer of much importance or relevance? To be fair, there are many churches or para-church organizations that have a significant work among older people but, generally, they are the exception. All too often, the older folk are required to be passive, to listen, drink tea, sing a few hymns, and go home: they have earned their rest.[1]

In this respect, the UK and other Western nations stand in stark contrast to Africa, for example. Two spells teaching in a Bible college in Kenya after my retirement from pastoral work in Scotland were an eye-opener. First, the Swahili word to describe an 'old man' is a title of honour and respect, and in no sense dismissive or condescending. Then there is the attitude of the Africans. 'Have you come, with all your experience, to help us? We are honoured!' You seldom hear anything like that in the UK, where it is assumed that, because of your years, you must be out of touch and any contribution you make must, inevitably, be somewhat old fashioned.

Some positive words penned by Georgina Bray in

her booklet *Ageing: A Sort of Ghetto-land* are encouraging: 'Old age and its symptoms need not be denied or felt to be a source of shame; it is a natural part of the life span, and a time in which God may be found as much as in any other time.'[2]

So, where do older people stand in the economy of God? The Old Testament in particular has many positive references to older people. Let's list some of them:

The righteous will flourish like a palm tree,
   they will grow like a cedar of Lebanon;
planted in the house of the LORD,
   they will flourish in the courts of our God.
They will still bear fruit in old age;
   they will stay fresh and green.   (Ps. 92:12–14)

Grey hair is a crown of splendour;
   it is attained by a righteous life.   (Prov. 16:31)

Grey hair [is] the splendour of the old.   (Prov. 20:29b)

She is clothed with strength and dignity;
   she can laugh at the days to come.   (Prov. 31:25)

Even to your old age and grey hairs

> I am he, I am he who will sustain you.

I have made you and I will carry you;

> I will sustain you and I will rescue you.   (Isa. 46:4)

This what the LORD Almighty says: 'Once again men and women of ripe old age will sit in the streets of Jerusalem, each with cane in hand because of his age.'   (Zech. 8:4)

These verses and others like them are full of promise, hope, encouragement and assurance. We do well to ponder them, especially when we feel depressed and low. However, it remains true that these isolated texts, and the truths they proclaim, are best illustrated by the actual lives of older people we meet in the Bible and by several of the psalms which are particularly relevant. That is what we have seen in the previous chapters.

SO, WHAT HAVE WE LEARNED?

- *From Abraham and Sarah:* no matter our age, we stand in a covenant relationship with a sovereign God. There is no age limitation when it comes to entering into God's promises and fulfilling God's call.

- *From Caleb:* the undoubted problems and challenges we face are to be assessed not by our own obvious limitations, but by the promises and power of God. Claiming God's promises is the way to confidence and assurance. There is no retirement in the life of faith. Fading may be the worldling's pleasure, but not that of the Christian.

- *From Naomi and Ruth:* humanly speaking, to an older person, so much that is good belongs to the past. No matter our situation and feelings, however, God is in charge of our lives. Intergenerational relationships can be deeply rewarding.

- *From Eli:* the passing years tend to bring a more tolerant attitude towards that which is wrong, and an unwillingness to take a strong stand. Doing nothing when faced with wrong, however, is not an option, especially if you are a parent. The consequences for all parties can be disastrous. Judgement will be severe for those who could have acted but did little, if anything.

- *From Psalm 71:* older people are sometimes made to feel that they are unimportant. Fears and doubts easily flourish. Yet there is immense strength to be found in the devotional habits of a lifetime and the rich experience of God which has been developed over many years. A backwards look detects the faithfulness of God in days past and gives hope for the future.

- *From Psalm 131:* it is pride that demands answers to the questions of life. We claim we have a 'right' to know and understand. The psalmist makes no such demands and claims no such rights. He turns from infantile insecurity, which frets when no answer is forthcoming, to quiet trust. We are to display not the fear of an infant, but the confidence of childlikeness. The Lord will give us our daily bread, even though he is unseen and, often, unfelt.

- *From Simeon and Anna:* don't dismiss the spiritual insights of the elderly! Consistent godliness, cultivated over long years, produces a special sensitivity to what God is doing.

Hope, sadly lacking in so many of advanced years, burns brightly in people of godly faith. The latter years of our lives could well be the most rewarding!

- *From Paul:* many in our day, if they think about it, approach death with a sense of fear. Yet the Christian, faced with the end of life, has a sense of thanksgiving and satisfaction. He or she anticipates that God will be pleased with a life of obedience and faithfulness. Our deaths will be a 'departure' but also an 'arrival'. Until that moment, we are to live lives of steady perseverance, holding on to the gospel which has been entrusted to us.

Notes

1 For an interesting and thorough survey of the situation, see **Ian S. Knox,** *Older People and the Church* (London: T&T Clark, 2002).

2 Cambridge: Grove, 1991.

About Day One:

Day One's threefold commitment:

* TO BE FAITHFUL TO THE BIBLE, GOD'S INERRANT, INFALLIBLE WORD;

* TO BE RELEVANT TO OUR MODERN GENERATION;

* TO BE EXCELLENT IN OUR PUBLICATION STANDARDS.

I continue to be thankful for the publications of Day One. They are biblical; they have sound theology; and they are relative to the issues at hand. The material is condensed and manageable while, at the same time, being complete—a challenging balance to find. We are happy in our ministry to make use of these excellent publications.

JOHN MACARTHUR, PASTOR-TEACHER, GRACE COMMUNITY CHURCH, CALIFORNIA

It is a great encouragement to see Day One making such excellent progress. Their publications are always biblical, accessible and attractively produced, with no compromise on quality. Long may their progress continue and increase!

JOHN BLANCHARD, AUTHOR, EVANGELIST AND APOLOGIST
Visit our website for more information and to request a free catalogue of our books.

www.dayone.co.uk

www.dayonebookstore.com